FROM GARDEN
TO GLASS

DAVID HURST

FROM GARDEN TO GLASS

80 BOTANICAL BEVERAGES MADE FROM THE FINEST FRUITS, CORDIALS, AND INFUSIONS

UNIVERSE

CONTENTS

WELCOME

Maybe you love the buzz of a good old-fashioned cocktail party, or want to impress your guests with a sophisticated alcohol-free drink over dinner. Regardless, the recipes within will help you rise to any occasion, whatever it is and whoever happens to be there.

Botanical tonics, tinctures, syrups, and infusions have a long history of being used as restoratives or for medicinal aid, and what better way to bring this tradition into the present than to twist them into delicious mocktails that bring the garden to your glass? In addition to tasting magnificent, they are full of vitamins and other natural health benefits, which are described in many of the recipe introductions.

All the drinks in this book can be enjoyed at any time of the year, but the whole idea behind this botanically inspired book is to let the beauty of nature speak for itself, and what better way to do that than by eating and drinking with the rhythm of the seasons? A juicy strawberry drink on a hot summer day? A restorative, warm spicy beverage in the chilly winter months? Perfect. Also, depending on where you live some ingredients may be difficult to access out of season.

An aromatic dash of spice here; a heady hint of floral there—it's incredible what you can create when you use fresh, natural ingredients. And now, I share these inspired recipes with you in the hopes of showing you just how much you can do with simple, beautiful ingredients, the right equipment, and a little know-how.

ALCOHOL-FREE ENJOYMENT

The drinks in this book are, by default, alcohol-free, but many can be made alcoholic by following the "Add a Twist" instructions at the end of the recipe. I've done this because so many people choose to abstain nowadays, whether for health reasons, athletic pursuits, or because they'd simply like a break.

In my experience, creating well-balanced and tasty virgin cocktails has always taken far more ingenuity. Nonalcoholic drinks have nothing to hide behind, and must rely on the quality of their ingredients to make them shine. The number of people who have cheerfully reported that my alcohol-free drinks "actually taste really good" has filled me with so much joy.

Cocktail books often categorize recipes by spirit, but this one is by main ingredient. I want to show you how versatile these natural ingredients can be, as well as make it easy for you to find a drink to satisfy your craving. Want a tangy and refreshing drink on a hot afternoon? The Citrus chapter is for you. The only chapter not organized in this way is Pitcher Party, which suggests several drinks that can be made in large batches.

Most recipes in this book serve one, but if a bowl, jug, carafe, or pitcher is mentioned, you have an ideal drink for a group. Other drinks that scale up are those that tell you to "top with" as this generally means you can make a large quantity of the base, divide it between glasses, add ice, and top up.

To get the most from this book, first read through the equipment needed and the glassware that is required; while you can start out with a few different types of glasses and build up your collection over time, you really need to have all the right tools of the trade before you can make any of the recipes.

As with any recipe, read through the method to ensure you have the time, ingredients, and equipment before you begin. Too many times I've thought how nice a recipe sounds and started to make it before getting to the part that says "chill for 6 hours"; not ideal when I'm expecting guests in an hour!

HOW TO COCKTAIL YOUR MOCKTAIL

Gin pairs well with apple, elderflower, and other herbs; try it in the Bee's Knees Martini (see page 77), or an Elderflower Collins (see page 38).

White rum is sweet so reduce the simple syrup in any drink you add it to; the mojitos (see pages 44 and 46), Lychee Daiquiri (see page 100), and Piña Colada (see page 92) are well-known white rum-based cocktails.

Whiskies and bourbons are caramelly, so a chocolate or dairy drink would be a good match; add a shot in a Blueberry Muffin (see page 142), a Vanilla Maple Shake (see page 64), or a Choc Orange Spice (see page 148).

Vodka is colorless and tasteless, so it's easy to add to cocktails; the Cosmopolitan (see page 121), Woo Woo (see page 117), and C Breeze (see page 118) are all classic vodka cocktails. Flavored vodkas speak for themselves: if it's a mango cocktail, simply add a measure of mango vodka.

Tequila is great with lime, so the Ginger & Peach Margarita (see page 54) and the Lime Sweet Station (see page 83) would be grateful recipients of a shot of the Latin American spirit.

1 FIRST THINGS FIRST

THE ART OF MIXOLOGY

What makes a great cocktail? Or should we first look at what makes a great drink? A vodka and orange, also known as a Screwdriver in the world of cocktails, would be served in a regular bar and charged at a price one would expect to pay for a spirit and mixer. The bartender pours the vodka into the glass then simply tops up with orange juice. The Screwdriver, on the other hand, although containing exactly the same ingredients, will be served in a striking glass, with plenty of ice, a straw, a stirrer, and a slice of orange on the rim. And the bartender may have shaken up the ingredients to wake the drink up and create a nice, lively, foamy head. For this presentation and theater, you'd expect to pay a premium. Seen another way, all he's done here is market the drink.

So how do you market your own virgin cocktails for your guests? Appeal to their senses. Admittedly, not every cocktail will smell amazing, as it may not contain herbs or fruits with strong enough aromas, but you can always make your creations look good and taste great. Many of them will have a comforting sound associated with them, whether it's the clinking of the ice against the glass or the fizzing of soda water; they may feel good to the touch, through the coldness of the drink or the shape of the glass.

However, before you even arrive at the stage of serving drinks that delight the senses, you need to look to the preparation stages. The art of crafting a cocktail, with or without alcohol, is akin to building a house: you need your land (your equipment and ingredients), then the building blocks (what you are going to put into the drink), and your tools (your shaker tin and other cocktail bar accoutrements). The garnishes, stirrers, and straws are the final touches—the soft furnishings, if you like. And just like building a house, you're best off sticking to the rules and making your first few builds simple but effective. Once you're confident in your ability to mix and match—and present (or market) your drink—you can be a bit more adventurous and go off the beaten track with your own variations, different types of glassware, and cool and gorgeous garnishes.

Learn how to make a few cocktails well, so that you know the whole procedure for three or four favorites. Once you're well versed in making these, you can be a bit more ambitious. Making a good cocktail well is always preferable to not quite getting an extravagant cocktail right. Just as a clean plate is the greatest compliment to a chef, so an empty glass is to a mixologist. Like any hobby, the main thing is to enjoy it. Hopefully, you'll learn something new while you're busy impressing your guests and enjoying the sheer variety of nature's flavors.

Try making variations on the cocktails you already know: a cocktail with strawberry in it should work equally well with raspberry or blueberry. Swap a garnish—it should reflect at least one of the ingredients in the drink you're making. Replace milk with cream in a dairy drink for true indulgence, or use sparkling water instead of lemonade if you want less sweetness. Two words: Be bold! After all, what's the worst that can happen? A drink that doesn't taste quite right, but at least you know which flavor combination doesn't work. You can put that knowledge to work next time.

TOOLS OF THE TRADE

Cocktail Shaker
Professional bartenders use a tin and a Boston glass, inverting the glass and placing it in the top of the tin. Aesthetics is the main reason: You can see the liquid being shaken. However, if you are more comfortable with a three-piece shaker, with a base, lid, and cap, go ahead and use it. The most important thing is to get the basic principles right and feel comfortable with whatever equipment you choose.

Jiggers and Measuring Spoons
A jigger, or thimble measure, usually comes in ¾- and 1½-ounce sizes. Measuring spoons, plastic or metal, are ideal for smaller amounts. In time, and with practice, you should be able to measure without using either.

Muddler
Metal, plastic, or wooden, small, medium, or large, they all do the same job. Use one to bruise or mash an herb or fruit, and wash it right away so it does not get clogged with old fruit.

Bar Spoon
A long-handled metal spoon, usually 1 teaspoon in volume, with a metal disc at the top end which can be used for muddling.

Strainers
A tea strainer or mini sieve is useful for separating solids and liquids. Professionals use a Hawthorne strainer, a metal implement comprised of a disc with a handle, and a spring around the edge of one side of the disc; the spring enables the disc to slot into the top of your mixing glass and strain out ice, fruit, and herbs.

Blender
Always add liquid first, then leaves, seeds, fruit, et cetera as it is kinder to the blades. Start on the slowest setting, then speed it up to purée the drink. Check if

the motor will withstand whole ice cubes; a less expensive brand will have no problem dealing with fruit but its blades will soon become blunted by ice. Worse, the machine will just give up completely. If opting for a less powerful model, use ready-crushed ice.

Ice Crusher

If your blender can't crush ice, look into buying a manual or electric ice crusher. A manual crusher should only be used when you need a small amount of crushed ice—it's hard work! Or there is always the rolling pin.

Pineapple Corer

A pineapple corer is a great piece of kitchen apparatus. It won't take up too much space and, although it has only one use, will serve you well. Not only will it enable you to get out a large amount of pineapple in one go, it also gives you a pineapple shell into which you can pour your drink.

Citrus Press

A manual press looks good and does the job, but is quite unwieldy. A better option, which takes up far less space and is much quicker, is an electric citrus juicer. Simply cut the fruit in half, hold it down on the plastic mold, and get the motor to do the work. An economical and essential piece for the kitchen.

Juicer

A juicer extracts the liquid from a fruit or vegetable and leaves behind the pulp. Because the juicer gives you only the liquid contained in the ingredient(s) used, it packs more nutrients in less volume than you would get with a blender, which leaves the fiber behind. Some argue that consuming the fiber is good, aiding digestion and making you feel fuller. Juicer versus blender is really a matter of personal taste.

GLASSWARE

First impressions matter. The analogy I draw for the significance of glassware, is that of someone going to an interview. When serving a large number of drinks, make sure the glasses are all of the same type. You may wish to lay them out so they form a circle, square, or triangle, for example, or arrange them so they form a letter

Casablanca	Hurricane	Martini	Coupe
A robust, ribbed glass; looks and feels like a very substantial glass. Ideal for anything you need to muddle and/or give a good stir.	Large stemmed glass with a fluted bowl shape. The Hurricane cocktail was invented in New Orleans containing rum and various fruit juices that required a large glass.	The archetypal cocktail glass, stemmed with a v-shape drinking bowl. Usually fairly low-volume glasses, whose ingredients contain quite strong flavors.	A stemmed glass often used to serve Champagne.

or number; the latter options are particularly effective when preparing drinks for a special occasion. On the other hand, when serving a smaller number of people, say between three to six guests, you may want to serve your drinks in different styles of glassware.

Margarita

This instantly recognizable glass is often used for cocktails such as the zesty margarita. This is also the glass of choice for frozen daiquiris.

Sling

Another stemmed glass, usually a much shorter stem with a "mini vase" on the stem. The sling came about when a new style of glass was wanted for the Singapore Sling.

Highball

The regular straight tall glass found in most private homes and bars/restaurants/hotels. Suitable for long drinks, mixed drinks, fruit juices, water, carbonated drinks, et cetera.

Old fashioned lowball

A short glass with a wide brim and a thick base.

INGREDIENTS

The "Essentials" below are just that—items I recommend you buy now and stock all the time. Anything you buy from the Essentials list is a good flavor investment as these ingredients appear frequently in the book, so it's worth it to re-stock whenever your supply gets low. "Particulars" are ingredients that are particular to only one or two recipes, and are therefore unlikely to be used very often. Many are either non perishable or have a long shelf life so all you're doing is building up your armory of ingredients.

ESSENTIALS	PARTICULARS	FRESH	SUNDRIES
Apple Juice	Agave Syrup	Basil	Serving Tray
Club Soda	Chocolate Syrup	Cardamom	Sip Stirrers
Coconut Milk	Goji Berry Juice	Cream	Stirrers
Cranberry Juice	Hazelnut Syrup	Crushed Ice	Straws
Elderflower	Melon Syrup	Cubed Ice	
Cordial	Orgeat	Lemons	
Ginger Beer		Limes	
Grapefruit Juice		Milk	
Honey		Mint	
Lemon Juice		Oranges	
Lemonade		Rosemary	
Lime Juice		Thyme	
Orange Juice		Vanilla Ice Cream	
Peach Cordial		Vanilla Pods	
Pineapple Juice			
Sparkling Water			
Simple Syrup			
Tonic Water			

MIXING IT UP

It's good to familiarize yourself with the following mixology terms before beginning. Most bartenders, most of the time, will use either the shake or stir methods. I do the same. Building, blending, and muddling are also covered here.

Shake and Pour

Shake all the components of the drink in a cocktail shaker, with ice, and pour everything into the glass.

Shake and Strain

Shake all the components of the drink in a cocktail shaker, with ice, and retain the ice in the shaker.

Stir and Strain

The ice goes into the glass, cocktail shaker, or jug with the other ingredients and they are all gently stirred together, then poured into the glass, with the ice kept back. Do this when vigorous shaking will bruise the ingredients.

Build

This entails pouring all the ingredients into the glass, which will already have ice in it, one after the other. Stir the drink well before serving.

Muddle

Use a muddler to extract flavor, usually from an herb or fruit. When muddling, it's important to remember that you are coaxing the flavor out of the herb or fruit by bruising it rather than bashing it into tiny pieces. You always need a little liquid to enable the muddling process, but don't add too much—it will splash you and also drown your fruits or herbs.

WATER AND ICE

Water

Tap, mineral, or spring? Distilled, purified, or filtered? Only to a well-trained palate is there any difference, so use what you have. The only big no is to use fizzy or sparkling when water is all that's called for.

Ice

First or last? Depends on your preference. If the ice goes into your cocktail shaker or blender first, then the ingredients you add cool the moment they hit the ice. Some mixologists argue that because the ice melts a little and dilutes the drink, this makes it a slightly inferior final drink. If you have freezing/chilling space available, use it! Ever been to a restaurant where the freezer they use to store the ice is very large, and it makes your heart sing? If you see this, you know that the drink-maker serves cold drinks cold. Keep your shaker tin, bar spoon, and strainer in the freezer, too.

The larger the cube, the more volume and therefore the more effective it will be. So if you have an ice cube maker or ice cube trays which make small cubes, consider buying large ice cubes or trays. Ice not only improves a drink's taste; it also feels good, looks good, and sounds good, too.

Most shaken recipes call for the drink to be strained over fresh ice. This is because the moment you hand it over, it goes into someone's warm hand who may be standing in a heated room or lounging poolside.

STOCKING UP

Here are a few pointers as to what you should stock to enable you to make a few drinks when the urge hits you or when surprise guests show up at your doorstep. And the more recipes you make, the more confidence you'll gain in trying out your own flavor combinations. It's a win-win scenario.

A few words on store-bought versus homemade: You can press or squeeze fruits to make fresh juices. You can produce your own cordials. You can blend your own fruit purées. There is a world of difference in a cocktail made from freshly squeezed limes or one from store-bought lime juice. Experiment. You are the best judge of what you like. I'm all for homemade but I'm also realistic, and know you have more pressing priorities than crafting an entire cupboard full of homemade cordials.

Fruit Purées
Blend fruits, such as berries, by washing them first, then pulsing them in the blender, gradually adding water so you achieve a consistency that makes them easy to add to the drinks you're making. You can freeze your homemade purées in sturdy freezer bags. Alternatively, good quality fruit purées are commercially available; most contain only 5 to 10 percent sugar. They are definitely not in the same category as store-bought fruit syrups, which have very little fruit in them.

Fruit Juices
Many of the recipes in this book contain juices that can be used in various formats. Take orange juice, for example: You can buy an economy concentrated juice or go up a level to a brand name; then you can move up another notch to

the freshly squeezed juice. Remember that store-bought fresh-squeezed juice has had to be transported many miles. To prolong its shelf life, it contains preservatives and other additives. The very best way of ensuring you have only the juice of the fruit—and nothing extra—is by squeezing it yourself.

Fruit Cordials

To make 33 ounces (1 liter) of fruit cordial you'll need about 2 pounds (1 kilo) of fruit (strawberry, raspberry, blackberry, gooseberry, red currants, black currants, or a combination of any number of these). Wash the fruit gently and put into a large pan with 2½ cups (500g) of sugar, 17 ounces (500ml) of water and the juice of 2 fresh lemons. Bring all of the ingredients to a boil and simmer for half an hour. Prepare a muslin bag by tying it to something so you can pour in the just-cooled mixture and let it drip through. (I use an inexpensive plastic tripod to set up my muslin bag.) This process should take around 90 minutes, after which you pour your homemade cordial into sterilized jars or bottles, seal them, and store them in a cool place, where they will keep, unopened, for two to three months. Once you've opened the bottle, store in the fridge and use within a week. Once you've done this the first time, the next is easy.

SYRUPS

You're about to embark on a journey from trainee cocktail bartender to master mixologist, I hope, so you might want to consider making your own flavored syrups. Some words of advice, however, before you start boiling, simmering, and cooling: homemade syrup will last around a month whereas the bought version will have a shelf life of around one to two years. It needs to be pointed out, too, that there is very little difference in cost between homemade and shop-bought.

Generally speaking, to make a syrup you need equal amounts of sugar and water, plus the flavoring, brought to the boil then to a simmer to coax the flavor out. Some syrups, and some palates for that matter, are more suited to a ratio of 2 to 1 in favor of water; obviously a syrup with less sugar gets a tick in the "healthy" box, but don't downgrade sweetness too much or it will become a detriment to the taste of the syrup. See below for a few recipes for some of the easier-to-make syrups.

Simple Syrup
This can be bought easily but it's so quick, easy, and inexpensive to make that maybe it should be the first homemade ingredient in your kitchen.

Put the same ratio of cold water to granulated sugar in a heavy-based pan and bring to the boil. As soon as it starts to boil, turn down the heat and stir well with a wooden spoon; you'll see that the liquid is gradually becoming clear and syrupy as the water absorbs all the sugar. Take off the heat. Leave to cool, then pour into a sterile bottle and store in the fridge. It will keep for a couple of months.

Stevia Syrup

Stevia is many times sweeter than sugar, so you can use less stevia syrup in recipes that call for simple syrup. It can be bought in its natural leaf format, as powder, or as a liquid. It's calorie-free, too.

Gingerbread Syrup

Put 1½ cups of superfine sugar, 7 ounces water, and 1 tablespoon of ground ginger into a saucepan. Add a cinnamon stick and bring the mixture to a gentle boil. Simmer for 5 minutes until the sugar has dissolved. Leave to cool and then pour into a sterilized bottle. Store in the fridge.

Cinnamon Syrup

Put 2 cups of water and 4 cinnamon sticks into a small pan; bring to a boil then simmer for 10 minutes. Remove the cinnamon sticks, bring the water back to the boil and add 1½ cups of sugar until it has dissolved. Cool and then pour into a sterilized bottle. Store in the fridge.

Chocolate Syrup

Put 2 cups of water into a small pan with a pinch of cinnamon and a couple tablespoons of cocoa powder; bring to a boil, reduce the heat, and simmer gently for 10 minutes. Bring the water back to the boil then add ½ cup of sugar until it has dissolved. Add an optional teaspoon of vanilla extract for interest. Store in the fridge.

Strawberry Syrup

Put 7 ounces hot water into a pan—don't boil it—and stir in 1 cup of sugar until dissolved; add 2 cups of strawberries, reduce the heat, and simmer for 10 minutes or so, stirring as you go. The syrup will reduce and thicken, and the strawberries will turn mushy. Cool, then strain into sterilized bottles and refrigerate. Store in the fridge.

GARNISH AND GLITZ

Apart from glasses, you need a continuous stock of straws, sip stirrers, and stirrers. You may still have plastic straws at home in a cupboard and want to use them, but do consider paper straws when buying new ones. If using plastic straws, they should ideally be the black bendy rather than the multi-colored, striped ones found in fast food restaurants. The smaller, much thinner straws, or sip stirrers (also called frappé straws) are so called as you sip through them and stir the drink with them. They are usually used in drinks served in lowballs, old-fashioned glasses, or martini glasses. (Longer ones would simply fall out of the drink.)

As for stirrers and themed events, you can really have some fun here. I've had events in the past where I've used stirrers in the form of tennis racquets and golf clubs, giraffes and cats, hearts and flowers.

Light-up ice cubes are lots of fun, too, and add a "wow" factor to an evening event. They are totally safe, and you only need one to light up a drink.

Lastly, you need different sizes and types of trays to serve from. Nonslip black catering trays will work well for holding a lot of glasses, but a small wooden or metal tray will suffice when you only have one or two drinks on offer. Think about going to a local market or second-hand shop and picking up some trays, which you can paint yourself in a rustic style or in bright summery colors. Very little outlay and just a bit of time will yield great results.

2 HERBS

ELDERFLOWER

BASIL

MINT & THYME

ELDERFLOWER FIZZ

1 teaspoon freshly
squeezed lemon juice

⅓ ounce homemade
elderflower and lemon
syrup

1¾ ounces red grape juice

Orange flavored spring
water

Sprig of elderflower
for garnish

ADD A TWIST

London Dry Gin plays
very nicely with the herbal
flavors in this recipe.

This delicious botanical drink uses an easy homemade syrup that is sure to impress. Elderflower, grape, and lemon are a classic combination. This drink can easily be scaled up for a summer party.

METHOD

Fill a highball glass with ice and add lemon juice, syrup, and grape juice. Stir to combine. Spritz the drink with orange-blossom scented water and garnish with a sprig of elderflower —I like to use a grape-colored sweet William, but anything from your garden will look gorgeous.

ELDERFLOWER COLLINS

INGREDIENTS

1 tablespoon elderflower
cordial
Juice of ½ lemon
¼ ounce vanilla extract
Sparkling water
Simple syrup
Slice of lemon, to garnish

ADD A TWIST

I like to add gin to
anything with elderflower,
as it brings out some
lovely floral notes.

Elderflower has been used in traditional medicine all around the world and in many different cultures. Ideal for treating colds and flu, sinus infections, and other respiratory problems, it can be taken orally as a rinse and/or as a mouthwash. It can also be used as a diuretic and laxative. Despite its antibacterial and antiviral properties, elderflower is also surprisingly sweet-smelling, a trait showcased in this showstopping drink. Its floral bouquet is a perfect match for the unmistakeable taste and aroma of vanilla. With a sweet and sour addition and sparkling water to add length and fizz, this is a delightful summer drink.

METHOD

Fill a highball glass a quarter full of ice cubes. Pour the elderflower cordial onto the ice along with the lemon juice and vanilla. Fill the glass two-thirds with sparkling water. Stir well. Add simple syrup to taste. If needed, add more ice and stir again. Garnish with a slice of lemon on the rim of the glass.

THE ELDER STATESMAN

INGREDIENTS

1 cinnamon stick

3 cloves

5 coriander seeds

3¼ ounces fresh pear juice

1 tablespoon fresh lime juice

¾ ounces elderflower
   cordial

Club soda

Lime wedge, to garnish

ADD A TWIST

Replace the elderflower
cordial with elderflower
liqueur for a cocktail that is
very low in alcohol.

This drink works because of how well the unexpected ingredients play off one another: the botanicals balance the elderflower; the pear brings the fruit factor into play; the lime points it up; and the soda gives the drink length and sparkle. Elderflowers themselves are wonderfully fragrant and the cordial they make has a grape-like aroma.

This drink requires advance preparation.

METHOD

Place all of the spices into a cocktail shaker. Add the pear juice. Leave to infuse for half an hour. Remove the spices. Add the lime juice, the elderflower cordial, and a handful of ice cubes. Shake well. Strain into an ice-filled highball glass. Top with club soda. Garnish with a lime wedge on the rim of the glass.

VICTORIAN GARDEN

INGREDIENTS

¾ ounces elderflower
cordial
¼ ounce fresh lime juice
2½ ounces freshly pressed
apple juice
Sparkling water
Slice of apple and wedge of
lime, to garnish

ADD A TWIST

For a sophisticated twist,
replace the sparkling
water with prosecco
or champagne.

This fresh, floral, and fragrant drink is perfect
for a balmy summer evening outdoors.

Homemade cordials are a fabulous way to
serve guests a drink that bears your personal
flair. Yes, it takes a bit of time to prepare a
homemade cordial (see page 29), but once
bottled, it keeps for ages. To make a standout
drink, simply add sparkling water, tonic, soda
water, or lemonade to a long glass filled with
ice and cordial.

METHOD

Add the elderflower cordial and the lime juice
to an ice-filled cocktail shaker. Pour in the apple
juice. Shake well. Strain into an ice-filled
highball glass. Top with sparkling water. Stir,
add a straw, and garnish with a slice of apple
and a lime wedge on the rim of the glass.

A BRUSH WITH BASIL

INGREDIENTS

6 fresh basil leaves
5 large strawberries
Dash of orange cordial
¼ ounce raspberry syrup
2½ ounces cranberry juice
Chopped strawberries,
    slice of lime and basil
    leaf, to garnish

ADD A TWIST

Gin or tequila would both
work well in this cocktail.

The slightly anise-like qualities of basil work well with the sweetness of fresh strawberries. For this drink, use regular sweet basil, as opposed to Thai or Greek, which are stronger and more peppery respectively. Basil is rich in vitamins A, C, and K, as well as magnesium, potassium, iron, and calcium.

METHOD

Muddle the basil leaves in the base of a cocktail shaker with the strawberries. Add the orange cordial, raspberry syrup, and cranberry juice along with a good scoop of ice. Shake well. Fine-strain into a chilled highball glass. Drop in some chopped strawberry, place a slice of lime on the rim of the glass and top with a basil leaf.

SPICED PEAR MOJITO

INGREDIENTS

10 to 12 mint leaves
3¼ ounces pear juice
3 lime wedges
¼ ounce simple syrup
1 tablespoon cinnamon
    syrup (see page 32)
1 ounce sparkling water
Sprig of mint and wedges
    of lime, to garnish

ADD A TWIST

For a spicy version of the
traditional Cuban, add
white rum.

A delicious combination of herbs, fruit, and
spice that awakens various areas of your palate.
If making your own cinnamon syrup, this is a
drink you can truly call homemade. Extra points
if the mint has been picked from your garden.

Feel free to vary the proportions to suit your
taste. For more tartness, add another lime
wedge. To sweeten, add more simple syrup, or
for more spice, add more cinnamon syrup.

METHOD

This drink is made and served in the same glass.
Place the mint leaves in a Casablanca glass and
add a drop of pear juice, just enough to wet the
leaves. Muddle for a few seconds. When you
muddle, you are bruising the leaves just enough
to coax out the flavor. Squeeze the lime wedges
into the glass and drop them in, followed by
the simple syrup. Mint, sugar, and lime—the
base of the Mojito. Add the cinnamon syrup
and stir. Fill the glass two-thirds with crushed
ice. Add the rest of the pear juice and sparkling
water. Stir once more. Add 2 straws. Garnish
with lime wedges and a sprig of mint.

MOJITO PASSION

INGREDIENTS

1 lime
2 passion fruit
1 green apple
1 cup cold filtered water
6 mint leaves
Crushed ice
Mint sprig, to garnish
Lime wedge, to garnish

ADD A TWIST

Add white rum for the perfect alcoholic version.

There is enough flavor in this virgin mojito that you won't miss the rum or sugar. Honest. You can swap the passion fruit for pomegranate seeds for a divine red mojito. This makes for another drink of starkly contrasting colors, as well as adding to the sensory impact: line up a few of these for a group of guests and they'll smell and see them as soon as they walk into the room.

METHOD

Cut the lime in half and squeeze the juice. Cut the passion fruits in half and scoop out the flesh. Cut the apple in half and discard the core and seeds. Place the lime juice, passion fruit, and apple in a blender with half the water and whiz for a minute until smooth. Put the mint leaves in a Casablanca glass and muddle (use a muddler, or a wooden spoon if you don't have one). Pour the juice over the mint. Add the ice and top with the rest of the water. Use the other end of your muddler or spoon to mix. Garnish with the mint sprig and lime wedge.

COCKTAIL THYME

INGREDIENTS

10 ounces (1¼ cups)
    granulated sugar

7 ounces hot water

6 sprigs of lemon thyme

7 ounces fresh lemon juice

2 wedges of fresh lemon

Soda water

3 slices of lemon and sprig
    of lemon thyme,
    to garnish

ADD A TWIST

A lemon-flavored gin is a great addition to give this drink some extra zing.

Thyme has a sweet, earthy taste and gives off the most wonderful aroma, so much so that it is widely used in aromatherapy. There are various types of thyme available for culinary use: Most frequently found in the kitchen is the regular "common thyme," though lime, lemon, and orange would be great variants to use here. Caraway thyme would give an aniseed-like flavor to this drink.

METHOD

First make the thyme-flavored simple syrup: Dissolve the sugar into a pan of the boiling water. Simmer until the sugar dissolves completely. Add the thyme and let stand for 2 hours. Add the lemon juice. Stir well and strain into a small jug or container, then chill.

Now, make the drink: In a cocktail shaker, muddle two lemon wedges with a couple drops of the lemon-thyme syrup. Add the rest of the syrup and a handful of ice. Shake well. Strain into an ice-filled highball glass. Top with soda water. Garnish with slices of lemon and a sprig of lemon thyme.

MINT & MELON MILK

INGREDIENTS

½ honeydew melon

4 ounces coconut milk

Squeeze of fresh lime juice

4 leaves of fresh mint

1 teaspoon runny honey (or
to taste)

Grated lime zest and sprig
of mint, to garnish

ADD A TWIST

A single shot of coconut
rum adds a slightly
alcoholic twist.

Bartenders love mint. It grows in most conditions, usually annually and quickly. And it's known the world over. Stick it into a garnish on the rim of a glass and your drink is transformed. Not only does it look great, it smells fresh, too. Use the leaf only as the stalks are bitter.

As with most of the recipes in the book it's best to chill your ingredients in advance. However, so often it's a case of just deciding on the spur of the moment that you'd like something that's cool, healthy, and tasty and uses up a certain ingredient, which may well be sitting in the fruit bowl or the cupboard; in which case let the ice take care of it.

METHOD

Quarter the honeydew melon, remove the seeds, then reduce the quarters to wedges. Cut off the rind. Chop the melon flesh into chunks and blend with the coconut milk, lime juice, mint leaves and a handful of ice. Add honey to taste. Pour into a highball glass, garnish with lime zest grated on the top of the drink and decorate with a sprig of mint.

3 SPICES

___

CARDAMOM
Coriander & Cardamom Tonic   52
Cardamom Martini   53

GINGER
Ginger & Peach Margarita   54
Earl Grey Lemon Mar-tea-ni   57
Ginger Zinger   58
Kooky Cookie   59
Spring Restorative   60

VANILLA
Vanilla Sky   62
Passion For Fashion   63
Vanilla Maple Shake   64

CORIANDER & CARDAMOM TONIC

INGREDIENTS

1 fresh vanilla pod

6 coriander seeds

3 black peppercorns

Sprig of rosemary

Strip of ginger

2 cardamom pods

½ cinnamon stick

¾-inch-wide strip
  orange peel

¾-inch-wide strip
  lemon peel

33 ounces hot water

¼ ounce simple syrup
  (optional)

¾ ounces fresh tomato
  juice

Tonic water

Wedge of lime and slice of
  lemon, to garnish

This fabulous-looking and -tasting tonic drink will make anyone still nursing a plain old gin and tonic feel like they're settling for second best—and they are.

You need your own "spicewater" for this, which can be produced in batches so you can introduce the liquid into other recipes in the book. Make the spicewater a day in advance as it needs time for the flavors to infuse.

METHOD

Add all the spices and the peels to a heatproof Kilner jar. Add the hot water and leave to steep for 24 hours. Shake gently to ensure the flavors are well integrated. Add simple syrup to taste. Once you have the infusion to your liking, pour the liquid into another jar, filtering out all the ingredients using a sieve, muslin, tea strainer, coffee filter—whatever gets out all of the liquid with none of the residue. Add 2 ounces of the spicewater to an ice-filled Casablanca glass. Add the tomato juice. Top with tonic water. Garnish with a wedge of lime and a slice of lemon on the rim of the glass.

CARDAMOM MARTINI

INGREDIENTS

5 fresh cardamom pods
¼ ounce simple syrup
1 ounce still water, chilled
1¾ ounces fresh
  pineapple juice
Wedge of pineapple and
  leaf, to garnish

ADD A TWIST

A pineapple- or orange-
flavored vodka gives a
welcome fruity addition
to this cocktail.

This is a tried-and-trusted formula with those old bedfellows of fruit and spice.

Cardamom is usually used whole, as the seeds lose flavor when released from their case.

METHOD

Muddle the cardamom pods with the simple syrup in the base of a cocktail shaker. Add the water and stir. Add the pineapple juice and a handful of ice. Shake well. Fine-strain into a chilled highball glass. Garnish with the pineapple wedge on the rim of the glass and float a leaf on top of the drink.

GINGER & PEACH MARGARITA

INGREDIENTS

1 teaspoon grated ginger
1 teaspoon white
   peach purée
Juice of 1 large lime
1 tablespoon orange cordial
Chilled water
1 teaspoon agave syrup
Slice of lime, to garnish and
   salt for the glass rim

ADD A TWIST

Make this a twist on the classic margarita by adding tequila.

What's a margarita without alcohol? A puddle of lime juice? Quite the contrary. Replace tequila with agave and liqueur with orange cordial and the drink is reborn. Add some gingery spice and this version rivals any after-work special.

METHOD

Put the grated ginger and peach purée in a blender. Add the juice of a large lime, the orange cordial, chilled water, agave syrup, and a handful of ice. Blend until the drink has the consistency of a slushie. Double strain into a coupe glass with a salt rim. Garnish with a lime slice on the rim.

EARL GREY LEMON MAR-TEA-NI

INGREDIENTS

Earl Grey tea
1 teaspoon finely
    chopped ginger
Juice from ½ lemon
¼ ounce simple syrup
1 egg white
Grated lemon zest
    for garnish

ADD A TWIST

Gin and ginger pair together nicely in a cocktail; you could also add interest with rye whisky.

The sharp, fresh taste of lemon and hot, spicy ginger are counterbalanced by the floral qualities of Earl Grey tea. The egg white gives the drink a rich and creamy texture and a frothy top. While complicated in its flavor profile, this drink is a cinch to make.

METHOD

Brew the tea. Let it cool with the bag still in the teapot; you want the tea to be strong and flavorful. Remove the teabag and pour the tea into a cocktail shaker. Add the ginger, lemon juice, simple syrup, egg white, and a handful of ice. Shake well. Double strain into a chilled martini glass. (Double straining ensures no pieces of ginger end up in the finished drink.) Garnish with lemon zest grated on top of the drink.

GINGER ZINGER

INGREDIENTS

Thumb-sized piece of
 ginger
1 banana
3½ ounces kale
5 leaves of lettuce
Sprig of parsley (curly or
 flat leaf)
5 leaves of rainbow chard
1¾ ounces (¼ cup) frozen
 mixed berries
7 ounces still water
Sliced banana for garnish

A little ginger goes a long way—it can keep for up to a month in the fridge, making it a good item to always have in stock in the kitchen. An added bonus: a thumb-sized piece costs pennies. It's both long-lasting and cost-effective.

I created this recipe while holidaying on the Isles of Scilly, where fresh fruit and vegetables are bought from "honesty stalls". (You simply leave your payment in drawers provided by the farmers.) Not only is this a wonderful way to shop, but it also leaves you in no doubt as to how fresh your salad ingredients are.

METHOD

Peel the ginger and banana. Blend all of the ingredients together. Pour into a highball glass. Garnish with slices of banana on the rim of the glass.

KOOKY COOKIE

INGREDIENTS

3 tablespoons caramel
 syrup
2 tablespoons heavy cream
2 tablespoons milk
1 tablespoon passion fruit
 syrup
1 tablespoon butterscotch
 syrup
Pinch of cinnamon powder
 and ½ teaspoon
 chocolate sprinkles
 for garnish

This sweet treat came about as a result of my two daughters asking if they could buy cookies for a train journey. I gave in and they both chose a different flavor. Having some time to kill on the trip, and keen to involve them in creating something fun, we came up with a flavor combination we thought would work well. When we arrived at our destination, we proceeded to mix them all up.

Here's the result, subsequently approved by grown-ups as well.

METHOD

Add all of the ingredients together into an ice-filled cocktail shaker. Shake well. Fine-strain into an ice-filled glass. Garnish with a pinch each of cinnamon powder and chocolate sprinkles.

SPRING RESTORATIVE

INGREDIENTS

1 green apple

3 celery stalks

½ cucumber

1-inch piece of ginger

2 kale leaves

1 lemon

A crisp green apple combined with ginger makes this a refreshing and reviving drink that can be enjoyed at any time of the day. The addition of kale means that this drink delivers quite the nutritional punch. Kale is full of antioxidants and is an excellent source of vitamins A, K, C, and B$_6$.

METHOD

Cut the apple into quarters and remove the core and pips. Add to the juicer along with the celery. Peel the cucumber, cut into thin lengths, and juice. Peel and add the ginger. Cut the stalks out of the kale and feed the leaves into the juicer. Peel the lemon, discarding any seeds, and add to the juicer. Stir well and pour into a champagne saucer to serve.

VANILLA SKY

INGREDIENTS

¼ ounce simple syrup

1 vanilla pod

2½ ounces freshly pressed
    pineapple juice

¾ ounces freshly squeezed
    pink grapefruit juice

¾ ounces coconut water

1¾ ounces bitter
    lemon extract

Pineapple wedge and leaf
    for garnish

ADD A TWIST

Dark rum is spicy and
chocolatey, making it a
nice pairing for this drink.

From sweet and sour to bitter and slightly nutty,
this drink delivers a delicious and exciting range
of tastes. The essence of vanilla has a lovely
aroma and undertone, and helps make it
a standout.

METHOD

First, make vanilla-flavored simple syrup: Put
the simple syrup into the pan. Split the vanilla
pod down its center. Add to the syrup, and
simmer for 15 minutes. Remove from the heat
and allow to cool.

Fill a cocktail shaker with cubed ice. Add the
just-cooled vanilla-flavored simple syrup along
with the pineapple and grapefruit juices and
coconut water. Shake well. Strain into a sling
glass half full of crushed ice. Top with bitter
lemon extract. Garnish with a pineapple wedge
on the rim of the glass and float a leaf on top
of the drink.

PASSION FOR FASHION

INGREDIENTS

2½ ounces hot water

2 ounces (¼ cup) granulated
  sugar

1 fresh vanilla pod

2 passion fruit

Juice from ½ lime

1 ounce passion fruit syrup

Slice of lime, to garnish

ADD A TWIST

Fruit-flavored vodka, such
as mango or coconut,
would work nicely here.

This standout drink calls for a bit of infusion time, so be sure to plan ahead before you make it. The yellow, juicy pulp of the passion fruit is quite sour and contains gelatinous seeds, which add a dramatic touch to the final presentation.

METHOD

Combine the just-boiled water in a pan with the sugar and simmer until the sugar is fully dissolved. Add the vanilla pod and muddle for a few seconds. Leave the mixture to infuse for a couple of hours.

Add the cooled, sweet vanilla mixture to an ice-filled cocktail shaker. Halve the passion fruit and scrape out the flesh. Add to the cocktail shaker along with the lime juice and the passion fruit syrup. Shake well. Strain into a chilled martini glass. Garnish with a slice of lime on the rim of the glass.

VANILLA MAPLE SHAKE

INGREDIENTS

5 ounces milk

2 teaspoons butter
   maple syrup

1 scoop vanilla ice cream

1 teaspoon almond extract

Finely grated dark
   chocolate, to garnish

ADD A TWIST

Whisky or bourbon would
round out this drink well,
adding a hint of caramel
and spice.

Most of our cupboards at home contain a jar or bottle of maple syrup; it can come out at any time of the day. It's a great addition to breakfast waffles or pancakes, and after-dinner ice cream.

Experiment with the additional flavorings until you find your preferred shake.

METHOD

Blend the milk, maple syrup, ice cream, and almond extract together, along with a scoop of crushed ice. Pour into a highball glass. Garnish with some grated dark chocolate on the top of the drink.

4 CITRUS

ORANGE

LEMON & LIME

GRAPEFRUIT

PAPA'S ORANGE FIZZ

INGREDIENTS

Juice from 5 large oranges
1 papaya
Sparkling water
Slice of orange, to garnish

ADD A TWIST

Try switching out the sparkling water for a light, dry prosecco for a twist on the mimosa.

Two kinds of papayas are commonly grown: One has sweet red or orange flesh and the other has yellow flesh. In Australia these are called "red papaya" and "yellow pawpaw" respectively. Another kind—picked green—is called a "green papaya," and is a staple in Thai cooking.

The colors of the drink and garnishes together are the picture of freshness.

METHOD

Pour the juice from the oranges into a blender. Peel the papaya and remove its seeds. Chop into chunks and add to blender. Blend well. (You may need to add a little water to get the right consistency—you are aiming for a drink as opposed to a thick smoothie.) Pour into a Casablanca glass. Top with sparkling water. Stir well. Garnish with a slice of orange.

BREAKFAST BOOST

INGREDIENTS

5 ounces freshly squeezed
   blood orange juice
2 teaspoons strawberry jam
1 ounce white grape juice
¼ ounce simple syrup
Juice from wedge of lime
Ginger ale
Fresh strawberry and slice
   of lime, to garnish

ADD A TWIST

Gin, vodka, or tequila
would all work nicely in
this fruity drink.

A delicious blend of flavors. Use homemade jam to add fresh strawberry to this mélange of different tastes.

Grape juices of all colors (red, white, purple, and black) are high in antioxidant vitamin C, though the white variety has the most refreshing and crisp flavor.

METHOD

Squeeze the juice from the blood oranges. Put the jam into a cocktail shaker tin along with the grape juice. Stir well to dissolve the jam into the liquid. Add the simple syrup, fresh lime, and a good scoop of cubed ice. Shake well. Strain into an ice-filled highball glass. Top with ginger ale. (Replace the ginger ale with ginger beer for added kick.) Garnish with a whole strawberry and a slice of lime on the rim of the glass.

MAI TAI

INGREDIENTS

2½ ounces orange juice

2½ ounces pineapple juice

Juice from 1 lime wedge

1 tablespoon orgeat syrup

Grenadine

Pineapple wedge, slice of
    orange, and sprig of mint,
    to garnish

ADD A TWIST

Add a shot each of dark
and white rum, or for a
cocktail with a much
lower alcoholic content,
simply substitute orgeat
for Amaretto.

The Mai Tai is a versatile cocktail that can be served long, short, or straight up. The orgeat—a type of almond syrup—adds a distinctly nutty flavor. Created by Trader Vic and featured in his restaurant in Oakland, California, the original drink features both white and dark rum. As rumor has it, the first lucky recipient of the concoction exclaimed, "Maita'i—Roa ae," Tahitian for "Out of this world! The best!" This nonalcoholic version preserves the drink's classic, almond-y tasting undertone and is strained into an old-fashioned glass full of crushed ice.

METHOD

Add the fresh orange and pineapple juices, lime juice, and the orgeat syrup to an ice-filled cocktail shaker. Shake well. Strain into an old-fashioned lowball glass filled with crushed ice. For a bit of color, drizzle a touch of grenadine over the top of the drink. Garnish extravagantly with the pineapple wedge, slice of orange, and a sprig of mint.

Homemade Lemonade
(see page 87)

TANGERINE DREAM

INGREDIENTS

5 large basil leaves
6 tangerine segments
1 tablespoon simple syrup
2½ ounces pink
  grapefruit juice
1 sprig of basil, to garnish

ADD A TWIST

Gin and citrus are lovely
together, and this
tangerine cocktail is
no exception.

The tangerine is sweeter and stronger than the common orange. It's also easy to peel and can be eaten on the go. Its name originates from the seaport of Tangier, Morocco, where the fruits were first shipped.

Note: It's a good idea to muddle the tangerine pieces first, then add the herbs to the mix and be a bit less frenetic in your muddling action. Gently does it.

METHOD

Muddle the basil leaves in the base of a cocktail shaker along with the tangerine segments and a drop of the simple syrup. Add the pink grapefruit juice, the rest of the simple syrup, and a handful of ice. Shake well. Strain into an ice-filled highball glass. Garnish with a sprig of basil.

BEE'S KNEES MARTINI

2 large oranges

Juice from ½ lemon

1 tablespoon peach flavored
  spring water

¼ ounce runny honey

½ slice of lemon, to garnish

ADD A TWIST

A shot of Bombay
Sapphire gin will enhance
the botanical flavors in
this martini.

With fresh lemon and freshly squeezed orange juice, and as good a honey as you have in the cupboard, this is a delicious drink to serve at social occasions or simply as a great pick-me-up.

I serve this cocktail in a martini glass, which ideally should be well chilled. Take a large scoop of crushed ice and fill the whole glass, or place a scoopful of ice cubes in the glass and add a couple of tablespoons of chilled water. Discard the crushed ice or iced water just before putting the finished drink into the glass.

METHOD

Squeeze the juice of two large oranges into a cocktail shaker. Add the fresh lemon juice. Pour in the peach water and add the honey, taking care to stir it all together and ensure the honey doesn't remain stuck to the base of your shaker. Add ice. Shake well. Strain into a chilled martini glass. Nectar!

CITRUS BELLINI

INGREDIENTS

1 tablespoon fresh
  lemon juice
1 tablespoon lime cordial
Sparkling water, chilled
Lemonade (see page 87)
Slice of lemon, to garnish

ADD A TWIST

The substitution of sparkling water with prosecco is the obvious choice here, as the classic Bellini and its variations are always made with prosecco.

This is a citrus version of the classic Italian cocktail from the 1930s, so it has quite a zip and zing. Giuseppe Cipriani of Harry's Bar in Venice invented it, naming it after the fifteenth-century Venetian artist Giovanni Bellini.

This is a great example of a family of cocktails: a "family" of well-known Italian artists' names have all been adopted as variants of the original Bellini. The Puccini has mandarin juice as its base and the Rossini uses strawberry purée, while the Tintoretto uses pomegranate juice.

The sparkling water may be enough on its own, especially if you like it drier. A few drops of lemonade provide added sweetness; it's barely noticeable but does add to the end result.

METHOD

Pour the fresh lemon juice and lime cordial into the bottom of a champagne flute. Top with sparkling water, leaving enough room for a finger of lemonade. Stir well but not too vigorously as otherwise the bubbles soon disappear and the drink loses its allure. Garnish with a slice of lemon on the rim of the glass.

SODA DAISY

INGREDIENTS

7 tablespoons tonic water
2 teaspoons grenadine
1 tablespoon lemon juice
7 tablespoons soda water
Slice of lemon, to garnish
Strawberries, to garnish

ADD A TWIST

This drink tastes great with champagne in place of the tonic water—perfect for a summer celebration.

Quinine, citrus, and pomegranate together provide an eclectic combination of tastes.

Grenadine is quite commonly used in the world of cocktails, gaining notoriety through the Shirley Temple, and is used to add both sweetness and color. A spoonful swirling around the surface of a drink or inside the glass adds a theatrical effect.

METHOD

Pour the tonic water into an ice-filled highball glass. Add the grenadine and freshly squeezed lemon juice. Stir well. Add another few ice cubes, stir again, and top with the soda water. Leave room for another cube or two of ice as well as a wedge of fresh lemon.

ROSEMARY LEMON COOLER

INGREDIENTS

1 ounce simple syrup
2 sprigs of fresh rosemary
1¾ ounces cranberry juice
Juice from lemon wedge
Soda water
Slice of lemon, to garnish

ADD A TWIST

Rosemary pairs well with gin, or to take it one step further, try switching out the soda water for prosecco. Careful—it'll be strong!

Earthy rosemary, fresh lemon, and dry cranberry form a terrific triumvirate of flavors. This infusion will need to be prepared well in advance of serving.

METHOD

Put the simple syrup in a pan that's already on low heat. Add one sprig of rosemary; the warmth of the syrup will release the oils and tease the flavors out of the herb. Take the pan off the heat and let the rosemary steep for an hour. Remove the rosemary and chill the syrup. Add the syrup to an ice-filled cocktail shaker. Add the cranberry and lemon juices. Shake well. Strain into a Casablanca glass with large ice cubes in it. Top with soda water. Garnish with a slice of lemon on the rim of the glass and a sprig of rosemary.

LIME SWEET STATION

INGREDIENTS

½ fresh lime
1 teaspoon honey
2½ ounces lemon-
    flavored spring water
Lime wedge, to garnish

ADD A TWIST

Add a measure of
Cachaça, the Brazilian
national spirit, for a
great take on the well-
known Caipirinha.

I made up this drink after getting off a train at Liverpool's Lime Street Station; I didn't have an alcohol-free drink to offer guests arriving in an hour. The station's shops provided the flavored water and honey. The venue's kitchen had a box of limes, and I crushed the ice with a rolling pin and tea towel.

This drink relies on the freshness of the lime and the quality of the honey. A warning: It takes a while to prepare. It's all about the stirring.

METHOD

Chop your half of lime into four, so you have four-eighths. Add two of the wedges to a sturdy old-fashioned or rocks glass. Muddle them well. Repeat with the remaining two pieces. Add the honey and a drop of the lemon water. Stir well. The honey will try its best to stick to the spoon, the lime, and the glass, but keep stirring and adding more lemon water until you have as much of it as possible mixed into the liquid. Add a scoop of crushed ice and stir again. Add another scoop of ice. Serve with two frappé straws and drop a wedge of lime into the drink.

SUMMER SUNSET

INGREDIENTS

¼ ounce fresh
grapefruit juice

1 tablespoon pomegranate
cordial

¾ ounces lemon juice

¾ ounces simple syrup

17 ounces sparkling water

2 x ½ slices of pink
grapefruit, to garnish

ADD A TWIST

Tequila and grapefruit are
a great duo, evidenced by
classic cocktails such as
the Paloma.

Pomegranate mixes perfectly with the citrus of the grapefruit, giving a delightfully effective sweet-and-sour combination. The health benefits of pomegranate are manifold: It's a good source of fiber and also contains vitamins A, C, and E, iron, and other antioxidants, notably tannins.

This is a sharp and refreshing drink; the sharpness will be toned down to an extent by adding the simple syrup, though adding too much detracts from the drink's characteristics. Best to add the simple syrup to taste.

METHOD

Put the first four ingredients into an ice-filled cocktail shaker. Shake well. Strain into a highball glass half full of crushed ice. Top with another spoonful of crushed ice and the sparkling water. Garnish with two half slices of grapefruit on the side of the glass.

GRAPEFRUIT BLAST

INGREDIENTS

3¼ ounces grapefruit juice
3¼ ounces orange juice
1¾ ounces lemonade (see
  page 87)
Slice of orange, to garnish

ADD A TWIST

As with any citrus drink,
gin would be a welcome
addition, adding a
pleasant herbal note.

This is probably the simplest recipe in this book
and certainly the quickest to make.

Grapefruit comes in different shades of pink,
red, and yellow and varies, too, in its acidity
and tartness, with some being slightly sweeter
than others. No matter the species or variety,
though, the grapefruit's sharp taste won't fail
to wake up your palate . . . or all of your senses
for that matter.

METHOD

Pour equal amounts of grapefruit and orange
juices into an ice-filled highball glass. Top with
lemonade. Stir well to infuse the flavors. (You
may want to add a couple more cubes of ice
and give it another stir.) Garnish with a slice
of orange on the rim of the glass.

HOMEMADE LEMONADE

INGREDIENTS

8 large lemons
6¾ ounces (scant 1 cup)
   granulated sugar
8½ cups water
Lemon wedge and sprig
   of rosemary (optional),
   to garnish

A great alternative to the commercially available versions, which bear little resemblance to the real McCoy and are often high in sugar content. This recipe will make a large quantity and can be used wherever a recipe calls for the addition of lemonade.

METHOD

Clean the lemons by scrubbing them in warm water. Use a zester or peeler to take the zest off four of the lemons, making sure there is very little of the white pith left on them as this will make your finished lemonade taste quite bitter. Put the lemon zest into a large bowl and add the juice from all the lemons along with the sugar. There's no need to strain out the seeds at this stage. Stir well. Cool in the fridge for at least 3 hours. Once cooled, strain into a jug so there's no zest in your lemonade, or, if you prefer, pour it all in, zest and all. Pour into ice-filled highball glasses. Garnish with a lemon wedge dropped into each drink and a sprig of rosemary, if using.

5 TROPICAL

PINEAPPLE

Pineapple & Kale Boost   90

Tropical Storm   91

Piña Colada   92

Singapore Sling   94

Paradise Cooler   95

Caribbean Float   98

Tropical Sparkle   99

LYCHEE

Lychee Daiquiri   100

COCONUT

Bermudan Breeze   102

Beet It!   103

Tropical Cream   104

Cocoda   105

KIWI

Kiwi Kooler   106

AVOCADO & MANGO

Green Light   109

Rise and Shine 110

PINEAPPLE & KALE BOOST

INGREDIENTS

2-inch slice of pineapple

3 kale leaves

½ cucumber

½ vanilla pod

Pineapple wedge,
   to garnish

Pineapple and kale may sound like an unusual combination but trust me, they work really well together. Zingy and fresh, with a hint of warmth coming from the vanilla. Replace the vanilla with fresh green chile for added warmth and spice.

METHOD

Slice the skin off the pineapple, remove the core, and cut the pineapple into cubes. Add to the juicer. Cut the stalks out of the kale and feed the leaves into the juicer. Peel the cucumber, add to the mixture, and juice. Scrape out the seeds from the vanilla pod; you only need a little to flavor this so add a tiny amount of the seeds and taste as you go, adding more if you like. Add 1 tablespoon of water and then pour into an ice-filled highball glass and stir well before stirring.

TROPICAL STORM

INGREDIENTS

2-inch slice of pineapple
½ mango
¼ melon
1 cup coconut water
Pineapple wedge and leaf,
   to garnish

Kicking up a storm, pineapple, mango, melon, and coconut are totally tropical bedfellows. In the case of a pineapple garnish, I always go for the wedge and leaf option, as the fruit is quite large and these parts of it won't be missed.

All the tropical fruits have high levels of vitamins A and C and manganese, which can be very useful in winter when other ripe fruits are scarce. If you buy the whole fruits, store any leftovers in the fridge and use as soon as possible; don't make up a large batch of juice because the vitamins and minerals oxidize quickly.

METHOD

Peel the pineapple, mango, and melon and coarsely chop the fruit. Place in a blender, add the coconut water, and whiz for one minute until smooth. Pour into a chilled highball glass. Garnish with a pineapple wedge on the rim of the glass and float a leaf on the top of the drink.

PIÑA COLADA

INGREDIENTS

1 small pineapple

3¼ ounces milk

1¾ ounces cream of
  coconut

Juice from 1 lime

1 pineapple shell, to garnish

ADD A TWIST

The most obvious addition here is white rum for an extra hit of tropical flavor.

The Piña Colada has been poured, shaken, muddled, and blended by bartenders the world over; opt for the blended version as this drink is all about the pineapple. The lime simply emphasizes the flavor profile.

This drink leads the way in over-the-top garnishes and over-embellished presentation. Here, you use the pineapple shell to serve the drink, carving a small hole for the straw. The garnish becomes the glass!

METHOD

Cut off and set aside the leafy top of the pineapple; this top will become the lid. Scoop out the flesh of the pineapple. (There are special corers you can buy but a stout knife works well.) Blend the flesh along with milk, cream of coconut, lime juice, and a scoop of ice. Pour into the hollowed-out pineapple shell. Make a hole in the lid wide enough to feed a straw through it. Place the lid on top of the shell. Enjoy.

SINGAPORE SLING

INGREDIENTS

1 ounce Morello cherry
    cordial
2½ ounces freshly pressed
    pineapple juice
2½ ounces freshly
    squeezed orange juice
Juice of ½ lemon
Dash of Angostura bitters
Sparkling water
Pineapple wedge, slice
    of orange, and cherry,
    to garnish

ADD A TWIST

The addition of gin here
creates the classic
well-known cocktail.

What at first looks like an odd selection of
ingredients becomes a harmonious balance.
Call it the magic of mixology: I'm not a fan of
some of the ingredients individually, yet I love
the end product.

This cocktail was popularized at the Raffles
Hotel in Singapore when the likes of Ernest
Hemingway stayed there. Today, most Singapore
Slings come pre-mixed and few bars serve them
with the style and elegance of a few decades ago.

There are so many variants that the author
of a 1948 book *The Fine Art of Mixing Drinks*
states, "Of all the recipes published for this
drink I have never seen any two that were alike."
Here's my interpretation of a classic.

METHOD

Pour the Morello cherry cordial into an ice-filled
cocktail shaker. Add the freshly squeezed
pineapple and orange juices, the lemon juice,
and Angostura bitters. Shake well. Strain into
an ice-filled highball glass. Top with sparkling
water. Add two straws, garnish with a pineapple
wedge and slice of orange on the side of the
glass, and top with a cherry.

PARADISE COOLER

INGREDIENTS

1 fresh guava
1¾ ounces freshly pressed
   pineapple juice
1¾ ounces freshly squeezed
   orange juice
Juice from ½ lime
¼ ounce grenadine
Pineapple leaves, to garnish

ADD A TWIST

An aged, dark rum would
add a spicy undertone to
the bright, fruity elements
in this beverage.

Guava has one of the highest concentrations
of antioxidants and is a rich source of fiber. A
guava a day keeps the doctor away!

METHOD

Peel the guava and remove its seeds. Put the
guava flesh into the blender along with the
pineapple, orange, and lime juices. Add a good
scoop of crushed ice. Blend. Pour into an
ice-filled highball glass and drizzle grenadine
over the top to create a bleeding effect. Garnish
with pineapple leaves.

CARIBBEAN FLOAT

INGREDIENTS

1 small pineapple

Large scoop vanilla
  ice cream

4 ounces sparkling water

4 ounces coconut milk

Pineapple leaves, to garnish

Fresh pineapple is a terrific fruit for dieters. It contains bromelain, a mixture of enzymes that helps digestion and breaks down fats and protein. Swap out the vanilla ice cream in this drink for a more low-calorie substitute and you've got a delicious treat for any "cheat day."

The hurricane glass is one you probably won't know by name but will certainly recognize from its distinctive shape. It's great to keep a few of these fabulous glasses on hand—they help transform any get-together into something, well, a bit more special. Guests love them.

If you do decide to go with ice cream, it's important that you use the very best you can get, as it will make a discernable difference.

METHOD

For this drink, you use the pineapple shell as the drink's glass. Carefully core and cut up the pineapple, leaving at least half of the pineapple shell intact. Place the flesh in a blender along with the ice cream, water, milk, and a scoop of ice. Blend well. Pour into the pineapple shell. Float the pineapple leaves on top of the drink.

TROPICAL SPARKLE

INGREDIENTS

3¼ ounces pineapple juice
¾ ounces lemon juice
Juice from lime wedge
3¼ ounces tonic water
Pineapple wedge and leaf,
   to garnish

ADD A TWIST

A shot of coconut rum is
a great choice to pair with
the pineapple flavor of
this drink.

The pineapple, or "piña" in Spain and "ananas" in Hispanic American countries, is versatile, with many health benefits. A ½ cup serving contains half the recommended daily intake of magnesium and vitamin C. It soothes coughs, sore throats, and upset stomachs.

This is relatively simple to make—just add the ingredients and give it a good shake. The trick is to make sure the ingredients have been mixed thoroughly. I prefer to add ice to the shaker first so that the ingredients can make immediate contact with the ice and are chilled right away. Other drinkologists add ice as the last ingredient so as to avoid the possibility of dilution. The choice, of course, is yours, and will depend on your personal taste.

METHOD

Pour the pineapple and lemon juices into an ice-filled cocktail shaker. Squeeze in a little lime. Shake well. Strain into an ice-filled highball glass. Top with tonic water. Garnish with a pineapple wedge on the rim of the glass and float a leaf on the top of the drink.

LYCHEE DAIQUIRI

INGREDIENTS

1¼ ounces lychee juice

1 ounce fresh lime juice

1 tablespoon black currant syrup

¼ ounce simple syrup

½ slice of lime, to garnish

ADD A TWIST

This daiquiri loves to team with white or golden rum.

Freshly squeezed lime juice is a key ingredient in a daiquiri. In the mining town of Daiquiri, Cuba, crude rum was given to malaria victims. The taste was disguised by adding fruity, zesty lime juice and, so that the drink didn't taste so sharp, sweetening it with sugar. And thus the daiquiri was born. In turn, various fruit flavors were added, the most common being the Strawberry Daiquiri. I have selected a more exotic fruit—the black currant—for added sweetness.

The daiquiri can be served in a variety of ways: straight up, short over ice, or frozen. This is the martini glass version. The short version is served in an old-fashioned glass over ice cubes. The frozen version is blended with ice, but only give a short blast on the blender so shards of ice remain in the finished drink.

METHOD

Add all the ingredients to an ice-filled cocktail shaker. Shake well. Strain into a chilled, frosted martini glass. Garnish with a slice of lime on the rim of the glass.

BERMUDAN BREEZE

INGREDIENTS

½ small pineapple

5 ounces coconut milk

Juice from 1 lime wedge

4 ounces ginger ale

Pineapple wedge and
  maraschino cherry
  for garnish

ADD A TWIST

Add a measure of
mango vodka for an
added measure of
alcoholic fruitiness.

The secret to this drink is ginger ale; it spices up the tropical flavor nicely. Ginger beer is a bit too spicy but, depending on your taste preference, you may want to give it a try, too. The coconut milk smoothes the concoction to perfection.

Note: Coconut milk is quite different from coconut water; its juice is extracted by pressing the grated white coconut kernel. It has a high fat content (24 percent); health-conscious individuals should consider using the light version. Today, both options are easy to find in supermarkets and online.

METHOD

Core and chop the pineapple and place in a blender along with the coconut milk, lime juice, and a scoop of crushed ice. Blend well. Pour into a highball glass. Add the ginger ale and stir. Garnish with a pineapple wedge and a maraschino cherry on the rim of the glass.

BEET IT!

INGREDIENTS

½ beet
Handful beet greens
4 ounces coconut water
Juice of ½ lime
Grated lime zest, to garnish

For this recipe, I use the root of the beet and the greens of the plant. With vitamins A and K, beets boost the immune system and support healthy bones.

METHOD

Scrub the beet and chop it into small pieces. Wash the greens. Add the coconut water and the lime juice to a blender. Add the beets and leaves along with a few cubes of ice. Blend well. Pour into a highball glass. Garnish with lime zest grated on the top of the drink.

TROPICAL CREAM

INGREDIENTS

1 ounce melon syrup

1 ounce freshly squeezed
orange juice

1 ounce heavy cream

¾ ounces coconut water

1 tablespoon peach cordial

1 tablespoon hazelnut syrup

Pineapple wedge and leaf,
to garnish

ADD A TWIST

Try adding a spiced rum
for a deeply delicious
nutty edge.

A smooth and creamy, fruity cocktail with a velvety texture. When you start a drink with dark green melon syrup, you know that the finished product is going to be fruity, tropical, and sweet.

METHOD

Add all of the ingredients to an ice-filled cocktail shaker. Shake well. Strain into a highball glass half full of crushed ice. Garnish with a pineapple wedge on the rim of the glass and float a leaf on top of the drink.

COCODA

INGREDIENTS

½ cantaloupe

¾ ounces coconut syrup

1¾ ounces freshly pressed
pineapple juice

1 ounce heavy cream

1 ounce milk

Pineapple leaf and wedge
and maraschino cherry,
to garnish

ADD A TWIST

As with most tropical
drinks, this could benefit
from a shot of rum.

This drink is based on a Samoan dessert that is made with coconut milk.

The cantaloupe, also known as the musk or rock melon, is one of around twenty-five varieties of melon. Its juicy flesh is orange-colored and sweet, and the seeds are relatively easy to remove. Melon is a fruit with numerous health-boosting properties. It's a wonderful source of beta-carotene, which is most commonly found in orange and yellow fruit.

METHOD

Cut the skin off the cantaloupe and put the flesh into a blender along with the rest of the ingredients, and a handful of ice. Blend for 30 seconds. Pour into a highball glass. Float a pineapple leaf on the top of the drink and, for added flair, garnish with a pineapple wedge and a maraschino cherry on the rim.

KIWI KOOLER

INGREDIENTS

5 ounces still water, chilled

2 sweet apples

½ avocado

3 kiwis

Handful spinach

Apple wedge, to garnish

Kiwis may be small but they sure pack a punch: They're densely packed with vitamins and nutrients, fiber, and protein. Also known as the Chinese Gooseberry, with its bright green color and black seeds, it certainly brings a bit of drama to a drink.

METHOD

Put the water into the blender. Core and cut the apples into quarters. Peel the avocado and remove its stone. Peel and halve the kiwis. Blend everything together along with the spinach and a handful of ice. Pour into a highball glass. Garnish with a wedge of apple on the rim of the glass.

GREEN LIGHT

INGREDIENTS

1 ripe banana

1 large, ripe Hass avocado

1 ounce plain zero-fat
yogurt

3½ ounces cooked spinach,
cooled and squeezed dry

2 tablespoons of agave
syrup

Handful fresh parsley

Banana slice and cubes of
avocado to garnish

For this recipe, the spinach needs to be boiled or steamed, so plan your preparations in advance. The cooking water will be packed with nutrients—you may want to let the liquid cool, store it, and include in your next smoothie! Or fill an ice cube container to use in cooking.

METHOD

Peel and slice the banana. Peel the avocado, remove the stone, and roughly chop the flesh. Blend all of the ingredients together, adding ice cubes until the mixture reaches your desired texture and consistency. Place a slice of banana and a cube of avocado on a toothpick or skewer. Drizzle both with a few drops of the agave syrup and place the decorated toothpick along the rim of the glass.

RISE AND SHINE

INGREDIENTS

2 tablespoons still water

2.12 ounces spinach leaves

1 mango

Juice from 1 large orange

2 teaspoons flaxseed

2 teaspoons cashew nuts

Sliced orange for garnish

It's fair to say that these recipe ingredients look more like a list of items for a breakfast bowl than for a drink. Flaxseed is commonly known as linseed and comes in a golden yellow color or a softer darker version. Both add little in the way of taste but they do bring texture, fiber, and omega-3. Flaxseed is also a great source of calcium, vital for developing and maintaining teeth and bones.

METHOD

Put the water in a blender. Wash the spinach leaves. Peel the mango and chop into chunks. Squeeze the juice from the orange. Add to the blender along with the mango, spinach, seeds, nuts, and a handful of ice. Add more water if the consistency isn't to your liking. Garnish with an orange slice on the rim of the glass.

6 BERRIES

BLOOD & SAND

INGREDIENTS

4 blood oranges
1¾ ounces cranberry juice
1 ounce peach cordial
Juice from wedge of lime
½ slice of blood orange and
   wedge of lime, to garnish

ADD A TWIST

To make this a traditional
Blood & Sand, add
scotch whisky.

This is a take on the 1980s classic Sex on the Beach (of which there are many variants.)

Blood oranges' coloring is due to an extra pigment. There are three varieties, of which the Moro is more commonly found in the US. They are stronger in taste than regular oranges and the skin is usually pitted as opposed to the smooth skin you see on regular oranges.

METHOD

Use the citrus juicer to extract the lovely deep red juice from the blood oranges. Strain the liquid into an ice-filled cocktail shaker. Add the cranberry juice, peach cordial, and a squeeze of fresh lime juice. Shake well. Strain into an ice-filled Casablanca glass. Drop half a slice of blood orange and a wedge of lime into the drink. The green, orange, and red together create a vivid palette of colors and make for a rather dramatic-looking drink.

CRANBERRY CRUSH

INGREDIENTS

2½ ounces orange juice
2½ ounces cranberry juice
¾ ounces ginger ale
Slice of orange, to garnish

ADD A TWIST

Gin or vodka are great choices for ginger and cranberry-based drinks.

This is one of my favorite drinks due to both its simplicity and taste—the dry cranberry and sweet orange combine well with the sparkle and length of ginger ale. I came across it in the 1990s and it's stayed with me. Takes seconds to make and goes down well with all ages and at all manner of functions. It also has a few variants: Top with lemonade for a sweeter taste, ginger beer for a sharper finish, or sparkling water when you want the focus to be on the juice. I prefer freshly squeezed orange juice to store-bought, though it adds to the prep time.

METHOD

Pour the orange and cranberry juices into an ice-filled cocktail shaker. Shake until the juices have created a nice frothy head, then strain. Pour into a highball glass three-quarters full of ice. Add the ginger ale. Garnish with a slice of orange on the rim of the glass.

WOO WOO

5 ounces cranberry juice
¾ ounces peach cordial
Juice from lime wedge
Lime wedge, to garnish

ADD A TWIST

The Woo Woo is traditionally a vodka-based drink. Try experimenting with different flavored vodkas for an extra twist!

Given its popularity as an alcoholic cocktail, this recipe, consisting largely of cranberry juice, shows off its efficacy as an alcohol-free counterpart. Laced with peach, the fruity, dry cranberry gets an added kick with a squeeze of fresh lime. The dry-sweet-sharp combo comes up trumps. It's the easiest recipe in the book, and one of my long-standing favorites.

METHOD

Fill a highball glass with large ice cubes. Add the cranberry juice and stir in the peach cordial. Take a wedge of lime, give it a squeeze, and drop the spent wedge into the drink. Give everything another stir, add a straw, and serve.

C BREEZE

INGREDIENTS

2½ ounces grapefruit juice

2½ ounces cranberry juice

1 ounce sparkling water/
   lemonade (see page 87)

2 x ½ slices of lemon,
   to garnish

ADD A TWIST

The cocktail version of
this drink has vodka as its
base; I suggest an orange
or mandarin vodka to add
interest here.

Is C for "vitamin C" or "cranberry?" In my book,
it's for "calm." The Sea Breeze, a vodka-based
cocktail, has its alcohol replaced with an
innocent yet sparkling topping. It's plain sailing.

There are several drinks that fall into "families"
of cocktails, each requiring the same basic
formulaic approach. The Breeze family, which
also includes Iced Teas, Rickeys, and Slings, is
made up of cocktails with two fruit juices that
create a new flavor as well as a new shade of
drink. Here, the dryness of the cranberry
mellows the tart grapefruit, while the finger of
sparkling water imparts some zing.

METHOD

Fill a cocktail shaker three-quarters full of ice.
Add equal amounts of grapefruit juice and
cranberry juice. Shake well. Strain into an
ice-filled highball glass. Top with sparkling
water or lemonade, depending on your taste
preference. Garnish with the slices of lemon
on the rim of the glass.

CRANTASTIC

5 ounces cranberry juice

1¾ ounces apple juice

½ fresh lime

1 tablespoon elderflower
   cordial

Club soda

Cranberries and lime
   wedge, to garnish

ADD A TWIST

Make this into a twist on
the classic Crantini by
adding a shot of vodka,
or take it one step
further and swap the
soda with prosecco for
a boozier version!

The dryness of the cranberry, the sweetness of
the apple, and the citrus hit of lime, combined
with the fragrant elderflower, makes this easy
to drink and easy to make.

METHOD

Add all the ingredients, except the club soda,
to an ice-filled shaker. Shake well. Strain into
a highball glass three-quarters full of ice. Top
with club soda. Garnish with cranberries and
a wedge of lime.

COSMOPOLITAN

INGREDIENTS

1¼ ounces cranberry juice

¼ ounce fresh lime juice

1 teaspoon orange cordial

1 teaspoon lime cordial

Orange peel, to garnish

ADD A TWIST

The alcoholic version found in bars across the globe contains a jigger of citron vodka.

Commonly known as the Cosmo, this classic contemporary cocktail was popularized in the 1990s and gained street cred as the drink of choice for *Sex and the City*'s fictional Carrie Bradshaw and friends Samantha, Charlotte, and Miranda.

METHOD

Fill a martini glass with crushed ice. While the glass is chilling, add all the ingredients to a cocktail shaker filled with ice. Shake well. Remove the ice from the martini glass—it should be nicely frosted. Strain the drink into the martini glass. Now for the dramatic effect!

Cut a round "coin" of orange peel, at least an inch in diameter, and hold it between your thumb and forefinger. Use a cigarette lighter or light a match with your other hand, and hold the flame above the orange peel. Twist and squeeze the peel over the flame to release the orange's essential oils. Drop the peel into the drink to impart a slightly burnt yet enticing orange taste. This garnish is just as much about the flair as it is about the flavor.

ROSEBERRY LEMON COOLER

INGREDIENTS

2 tablespoons simple syrup

Sprig of fresh rosemary

3½ tablespoons cranberry
    juice

Juice from lemon wedge

Soda water

Sprig of rosemary and
    lemon slice for garnish

Earthy rosemary, fresh lemon, and dry cranberry form a terrific trio of flavors.

Note: This infusion will also need to be prepared well in advance of serving.

METHOD

Put the simple syrup in a pan that's already on low heat. Add the sprig of rosemary; the warmth of the syrup will release the oils and tease the flavors out of the herb. Take the pan off the heat and let the rosemary steep for an hour. Remove the rosemary and chill the mixture. Add the syrup to an ice-filled cocktail shaker. Add the cranberry and lemon juices. Shake well. Strain into a Casablanca glass with large ice cubes in it. Top with soda water. Garnish with a lemon slice on the rim of the glass and a sprig of rosemary.

APRICOT APPETIZER

INGREDIENTS

2 apricots

3½ ounces fresh
strawberries

7 tablespoons freshly
squeezed orange juice

3½ tablespoons sparkling
water

Orange slice and
strawberry for garnish

Apricots have been cultivated since antiquity, and dried ones were an important commodity on Persian trade routes. Sweet and fragrant, golden-orange apricots remain an important fruit in modern-day Iran where they are known under the common name of Zard-ālū. The Greeks were the first to bring them to Europe and called them the "golden eggs of the sun."

Because the skin is edible and tasty, it's possible to make this drink with the skin washed and left on. It comes down to the texture of the drink and the power of your blender; a lot of the modern, more compact, blenders have an extremely powerful action that blitzes everything (within reason) that you put into it. If your machine isn't one of these types then you may not want to serve this drink with little bits of skin in it that haven't been totally pulverized.

METHOD

Remove the apricot stones. Rinse, hull, and slice the strawberries. Blend all of the fruit and orange juice together along with a scoop of crushed ice. Pour into a highball glass. Top with a little sparkling water before giving the drink a final stir. Garnish.

RASPBERRY RAZZLE

INGREDIENTS

12 fresh raspberries

1 scoop vanilla ice cream

¾ ounces heavy cream

1¾ ounces raspberry cordial

¼ ounce lime cordial

2 fresh raspberries
for garnish

ADD A TWIST

The slightly sour fruitiness of the raspberry would be nicely complemented by the addition of vanilla vodka.

Sharp and sweet at the same time, this drink makes for a fabulous dessert.

METHOD

Wash the raspberries. Blend together with the vanilla ice cream, heavy cream, the raspberry and lime cordials, and a scoop of ice. Pour into a Casablanca glass. Float two raspberries on the top of the drink.

LETTUCE EAT BERRIES

INGREDIENTS

Juice from 2 large oranges
4 large strawberries
Handful frozen blueberries
2 teaspoons chia seeds
½ head of iceberg lettuce
2½ ounces low-fat plain
  yogurt
Orange slice for garnish

Smoothies can be a great way of cleaning out the fridge and putting to good use leftover salads, fruits, and vegetables. Even putting a small amount of each in the compost bin can feel like a waste of money. Rather than throwing out leftover iceberg lettuce, I threw it in this mix instead. I've been so pleased with the end result, I've taken to saving lettuce just to make this drink.

Note: Frozen blueberries go in this mix so we don't need ice.

METHOD

Squeeze the oranges and pour the fresh juice into the blender. Blend with the rest of the ingredients. Pour into a highball glass. Garnish with an orange wheel on the rim of the glass.

FRUIT SPIRAL

INGREDIENTS

3½ ounces iceberg lettuce

3 fresh large strawberries

⅔ cup soy milk

2 teaspoons of spirulina

1 banana

Sliced strawberry
   for garnish

Spirulina is a natural algae powder packed with antioxidants, protein, vitamins A, B, and C, and iron.

METHOD

Wash and chop the lettuce and strawberries. Blend along with the soy milk, spirulina, banana, and a handful of ice. Pour into a highball glass. Garnish with a slice of strawberry.

BERRY BLAST

INGREDIENTS

6 fresh raspberries

6 fresh strawberries

6 fresh blueberries

6 fresh blackberries

1 ounce elderflower cordial

Juice from 1 lime

¼ ounce simple syrup

Ginger beer

Fresh berries and metal
cocktail stick, to garnish

ADD A TWIST

Lemon-flavored vodka
would transform this
into a spin-off on
berry lemonade.

One of the most popular cocktails in the world, the Mojito requires a muddler to gently bruise the mint and coax out the flavors from the leaves. With this drink, there's no coaxing of flavors per se but, instead, a barbaric bashing of berries to turn them into a fabulously fresh purée. The aroma is wonderful and hints at the drink that is to come.

Note: Take care to point the shaker away from you when making this drink, so you don't end up with stained clothes from errant berry juices.

METHOD

Muddle the berries in the base of a cocktail shaker. Squeeze in the fresh lime juice. Add the simple syrup, cordial, and a handful of ice cubes. Shake well. Strain into handled jars filled with crushed ice. Top with ginger beer. Spear extra berries on a metal cocktail pick and lay across the top of the glass to garnish.

KALE & STRAWBERRY SMOOTHIE

INGREDIENTS

3½ ounces kale

6 fresh large strawberries

1¾ low-fat plain yogurt

2 tablespoons skim milk

2 teaspoons runny honey
   (or to taste)

Thinly sliced strawberry
   for garnish

Frozen fruits can be just as good for you as the non-frozen variety. The fruits' nutrients have been locked in not long after the fruit has been picked. Most fresh fruit withstands lots of travel time and has been sitting on the shelf before making its way into your kitchen. Stock up on frozen fruits. They have the added benefit of providing the ice factor if you run out of cubes.

METHOD

Blend the kale and strawberries, along with the yogurt, milk, and a handful of ice. Add the honey to taste. Garnish with strawberry slices on the top of the drink and eat them as you drink.

BERRY NICE

INGREDIENTS

Handful fresh raspberries

3½ tablespoons still water, chilled

3½ tablespoons orange juice

4 teaspoons raspberry cordial

1 teaspoon light cream

1 teaspoon simple syrup

1 raspberry for garnish

This drink can double as dessert.

Apart from the usual red and purple raspberries, they can also be found in black and gold, the gold ones being exceptionally sweet.

METHOD

Add a handful of ice to a martini glass and leave it to chill while you prepare the drink. Blend the raspberries with water for 10 seconds. Pour the fresh raspberry liquid into an ice-filled cocktail shaker along with the other ingredients. Shake well. Strain into the chilled martini glass. Garnish with a raspberry dropped into the drink.

FRUITS OF THE FOREST

INGREDIENTS

10 fresh blackberries

10 fresh raspberries

1 tablespoon blackberry
cordial

1 tablespoon raspberry
cordial

2½ ounces cranberry juice

1 ounce still water

Juice of 1 lime

Club soda

1 blackberry and 1
raspberry, to garnish

ADD A TWIST

Pimm's No. 1 liqueur
would be a lovely
addition here.

For many of us, childhood memories entail picking blackberries and raspberries and making jams, jellies, or pies with them. Reminisce and relive those days with this fresh and fruity berry delight. Both berries are rich in vitamins C and K and omega-3, and help to give this drink a healthy kick.

METHOD

Muddle the berries in the base of a cocktail shaker. Add the cordials, cranberry juice, water, lime juice, and a generous handful of ice. Shake well. Strain into a highball glass half full of ice. Top with club soda. Float the raspberry and blackberry on the top of the drink.

STRAWBERRY MULE

INGREDIENTS

Piece of fresh ginger

Slice of fresh red chile
  pepper (seeds removed)

1 teaspoon simple syrup

¾ ounces fresh
  strawberry purée

Juice of ½ lime

Ginger beer

Lime wedge and strawberry,
  to garnish

ADD A TWIST

If you dare, add even
more spice with a slug of
spiced rum.

Our take on the ubiquitous Moscow Mule, which derives its name from the "kick" of the ginger beer, and the city of Moscow, since Russia was long associated with vodka. Fresh strawberry and lime sweeten the drink, add some color and vibrancy, and counterbalance the heat. Experiment with the amount of chile and ginger you use. Personally, I use more than what's listed; I love the invasion of heat after the initial sweet and fizzy combo of the strawberry-ginger.

With sweet and sour, fire and ice, and red and green, this is another drink that will draw ooohs and aaahs from your guests.

METHOD

Using a muddler or the flat disc end of a bar spoon, muddle together a thumb-sized piece of fresh ginger with a one-inch slice of chile, and simple syrup in the base of a cocktail shaker. Add the strawberry purée, the lime juice, and a good scoop of ice. Shake all the ingredients together and double strain into an ice-filled highball glass. Top with the ginger beer. Garnish with a lime wedge and strawberry on the rim of the glass.

SUMMER RAIN

INGREDIENTS

2⅔ ounces (⅜ cup) fresh
 strawberries
Juice from 5 large oranges
1¾ ounces lemonade
Juice from 2 lime wedges
Lime wedge and strawberry,
 to garnish

ADD A TWIST

Add a measure of vodka to
turn this into a "Summer
Storm".

Packed with the taste of summer and given
length and sparkle by the addition of lemonade,
this drink is as colorful as it is fresh and vibrant.

In many of these recipes the question of fresh
juice versus concentrate is open to interpretation
and personal preference. Here, however, the
orange juice needs to be freshly squeezed.

The berries and the citrus are all prepared
from scratch, so this drink is as fresh as can be.
Strawberries are packed full of health-boosting
vitamins C and K, as well as antioxidants.

METHOD

Rinse, hull, and slice the strawberries. Squeeze
the oranges and blend the juice along with the
strawberries and a handful of crushed ice. Pour
into a highball glass with a few ice cubes. Top
with the lemonade and the lime juice. Drop
the spent wedges into the drink. Perch a lime
wedge on the rim of the glass along with a
fresh strawberry.

BLUEBERRY & GINGER CUP

INGREDIENTS

Handful blueberries

¼ ounce fresh lemon juice

1 tablespoon vanilla extract

¼ ounce simple syrup

¼ ounce fresh ginger juice

2½ ounces cranberry juice

Blueberries, ½ slice of
lemon, and ½ slice of
lime, to garnish

Made with fresh blueberries, lemon juice, ginger, and cranberry, this drink is a pleasant assault on the senses. The fresh berries and citrus give a lovely aroma; the drink itself is a beautiful, deep red color with a garnish of yellow and blue; the ice provides a satisfying crunch; and the taste is wonderful.

Blueberries are a known source of vitamins C and K and provide the body with a good supply of antioxidants, benefitting the brain and the nervous system. Scientific research proves that blueberries not only help improve memory function, but they also slow the onset of problems associated with aging.

METHOD

Place the blueberries in the base of a cocktail shaker and add the lemon juice. Muddle together. Add the vanilla, simple syrup, ginger juice, and a large scoop of ice. Shake well. Fill a Casablanca glass two-thirds with crushed ice. Strain into the glass. Add the cranberry juice. Stir well. Top with more crushed ice. Drop a few blueberries and the slices of lemon and lime into the drink.

NUTTY GOJI MARTINI

INGREDIENTS

5 ounces goji berry juice
1½ tablespoons orgeat
Sparkling water
Lime wedge, to garnish

ADD A TWIST

Pair the orgeat, which is used in many tropical drinks, with rum for an even more tropical flavor.

Dried goji berries look and taste like, and can be used in the same way as, dried cranberries. They've been grown, cultivated, eaten and drunk in the Himalayas and China for centuries. There are vastly exaggerated claims but what is not disputed is that the iron-rich berries *do* contain beneficial vitamins and nutrients like zinc, potassium, selenium, and vitamins A and C.

METHOD

Pour the goji berry juice into an ice-filled shaker. Add the orgeat. Shake well. Strain into an ice-filled Casablanca glass. Top with sparkling water. Garnish with a wedge of lime on the rim of the glass.

AÇAI & MELON MARTINI

INGREDIENTS

2 large slices watermelon
2½ ounces açai berry juice
1 ounce freshly pressed
   apple juice
1 tablespoon fresh
   lime juice
Apple and watermelon
   slices, to garnish

ADD A TWIST

A slug of golden rum
would add a little caramel
sweetness to these lovely
tropical flavors.

When the açai berry moved out of the Brazilian rainforest and into the city, largely due to surfers and sporting aficionados who extolled the berry's many virtues and gulped down the fruit on a daily basis, the world of food science took note. The popularity of the açai berry is due to its amino acids, which help muscles perform and aid endurance and stamina. These purple berries are also rich in antioxidants, essential fatty acids, and vitamins A, B, and E, and are a great source of magnesium, zinc, copper, and calcium. No wonder the açai berry has been elevated to the status of superfood.

METHOD

Cut away the flesh from the skin of the watermelon and remove as many of the seeds as possible. Muddle the watermelon in the base of a cocktail shaker. Add the açai berry juice, apple juice, and the freshly squeezed lime. Fill with ice cubes. Shake well. Double strain into a chilled martini glass. Garnish with apple and watermelon slices on the side of the glass.

BLUEBERRY MUFFIN

Handful blueberries

¼ ounce fresh lemon juice

1 tablespoon vanilla extract

¼ ounce simple syrup

¼ ounce gingerbread syrup
(see page 32)

2½ ounces cranberry juice

Blueberries and a slice of
lemon, to garnish

ADD A TWIST

Bourbon or whisky would
add a nice caramel flavor,
making this cocktail
taste even more like a
blueberry muffin.

This is a delicious after-dinner drink or perfect as part of an indulgent afternoon tea.

Blueberries are an excellent source of vitamins C and K and useful antioxidants, which benefit the brain and the nervous system.

METHOD

Place the blueberries in the base of a cocktail shaker and add the lemon juice. Muddle together. Add the vanilla, simple syrup, gingerbread syrup, and a large scoop of ice. Shake well. Fill a Casablanca glass two-thirds with crushed ice. Strain into the glass. Add the cranberry juice. Stir well. Top with more crushed ice. Add two straws. Spear blueberries on a metal cocktail pick and lay across the top of the glass. Add the slice of lemon to the rim of the glass.

AÇAI BREEZE

2½ ounces cranberry juice

2½ ounces açai berry juice

1¾ ounces apple juice

Slices of lemon, to garnish

ADD A TWIST

If you want to add alcohol to this drink, vodka would be the natural choice to offset the powerful berry flavors.

These purple berries look like grapes and often taste like red wine. Because of its many virtues, the açai berry is often marketed as an "ultra premium superfood." A plentiful source of iron, the berries also contain vitamins A, B_1, B_2, B_3, and E, as well as fatty and amino acids, and they are antioxidant-rich—good for body, mind, and soul.

Note: For this recipe, it's important to use large ice cubes as they take longer to melt.

METHOD

Fill a highball glass with large ice cubes. Stir all the ingredients together well, then add more ice if it has reduced in size. Garnish with a couple slices of lemon dropped into the drink.

LINGER ON

INGREDIENTS

7 tablespoons lingonberry
  juice
7 tablespoons grapefruit
  juice
Juice from lime wedge
Ginger ale
Lime slice for garnish

Lingonberries—the Scandinavian equivalent of blackberries—are a smaller cousin of the cranberry. Indeed, they are known as mountain cranberries and partridge berries in the parts of North America where they can be found.

It's a quite bitter and sour fruit, so with this cocktail also containing grapefruit juice and fresh lime, you can see where we'll end up with the overall taste. Sharp and with quite a kick, this is a real pick-me-up.

METHOD

Pour the juices into an ice-filled shaker. Shake well. Strain into an ice-filled highball glass. Top with ginger ale. Garnish with a lime slice on the rim of the glass.

7 BEANS

COCOA

COFFEE

CHOC ORANGE SPICE

INGREDIENTS

2½ ounces whole milk

1 cinnamon stick

¼ ounce freshly squeezed
   orange juice

1 tablespoon chocolate
   syrup (see page 32)

1 ounce heavy cream

Grated nutmeg and cocoa
   powder, to garnish

ADD A TWIST

The injection of a smoky
single malt whiskey to this
flavor combo would be
ideal here; we all know
how well chocolate and
whisky pair up together.

A drink for the chocaholics among us, complete
with chocolate syrup, cocoa powder, and
sprinkles! The type of milk you use—whole,
low-fat, skim, or fat-free—is dependent on your
own taste and preference. For this particular
recipe, however, I recommend using whole milk
for extra creaminess.

METHOD

Slowly heat the milk in a small pan with the
cinnamon stick. Gently simmer for 2 to 3
minutes to bring out the spice of the cinnamon
stick. Leave to cool, then remove the cinnamon
stick. Add the spiced milk to an ice-filled
cocktail shaker along with the orange juice,
chocolate syrup, and heavy cream. Shake well.
Fill an old-fashioned glass halfway with crushed
ice. Strain into the glass. Garnish with a pinch
of grated nutmeg and cocoa powder.

VIVA EL CHOCTEL!

INGREDIENTS

1 young coconut or 2 cups
  coconut milk
1 small red or green
  chile pepper
½-inch vanilla pod
1 cardamom seed
2–3 tablespoons raw
  cacao powder
Sea or rock salt

ADD A TWIST

Add a shot of white creme de cacao to up the chocolate stakes.

The word "cocktail" in Spanish is "coctel", so I introduced an "h" into both words and created a new word; wholly self-explanatory.

Make a creamy chocolate drink using the water and flesh of a young coconut (or use coconut milk if you prefer). Raw cacao adds a chocolate hit and chile, cardamom, and salt combine to lift the whole thing into something really special.

METHOD

If using a fresh coconut, cut it open, catching all the milk. Scrape out the flesh. Put the flesh and milk (or coconut milk, if using) into a blender. Cut open the chile, scrape out and discard the seeds. Crush lightly with the back of a knife and add as much as you like to the blender (you can always add more at the end). Cut open and crush the vanilla pod and add to the blender. Bash the cardamom seed with a wooden spoon to release the oils. Put the cardamom seed and cacao powder into the blender and whiz everything for a minute until smooth. Add a little salt to taste. Pour into a highball glass to serve.

BANOFFEE & PASSION SHAKE

INGREDIENTS

3 pieces dark chocolate

3 pieces milk chocolate

1 fresh vanilla pod

2½ ounces milk

1 dessert spoon
   superfine sugar

1 ounce toffee sauce

¼ ounce banana syrup

¼ ounce butterscotch
   syrup

1 ounce half-and-half

1 fresh passion fruit

Banana slice, to garnish

ADD A TWIST

For a low-alcohol addition
to this drink, introduce a
measure of passion fruit
liqueur to the shaker.

Passion fruit adds a delicious tartness to this interesting cocktail, which perfectly counteracts some of the sweetness of the other ingredients. Its flesh and seeds also make it uniquely pretty.

METHOD

Place chocolate in a small heatproof bowl. Bring about an inch of water to simmer in a saucepan or pot. Set the bowl in the mouth of the pot, making sure the water doesn't touch the bottom of the bowl. Stir the chocolate as it melts. Carefully coat the inside of the martini glass with the melted chocolate for a marbled effect. Chill the glass.

Make the vanilla milk: Split the vanilla pod, remove its seeds, and add both to a small pan with the milk. Slowly heat the milk to boiling. Remove from heat and leave to cool. Strain out the pod and seeds. Halve the passion fruit and scoop out the flesh. Pour the vanilla milk along with the rest of the ingredients into an ice-filled cocktail shaker. Shake well. Strain into the chocolate-decorated martini glass. Garnish with a banana slice on the rim.

ESPRESSO MARTINI

INGREDIENTS

4 to 5 ounces cold
espresso coffee

1 ounce caramel syrup

1 tablespoon simple syrup
(or to taste)

3 coffee beans, to garnish

ADD A TWIST

Try this with an espresso-
flavored vodka for an even
richer coffee taste.

This Espresso Martini is a take on the vodka-based contemporary classic. With its handsome, creamy foam top and its dark-brown body, this two-toned, caffeine-fueled cocktail is the perfect after-dinner drink. While it can be made with instant coffee, it's best to use freshly ground coffee beans. For the ultimate pick-me-up, serve this as shots.

METHOD

Pour 10 ounces of boiling water into a French press containing 2 teaspoons of coffee (instant or freshly ground). Stir and leave for 5 minutes. Stir again, then plunge and leave for another 5 minutes before pouring the coffee into a mug. Leave to cool.

Put the cold coffee into an ice-filled cocktail shaker. Add the caramel syrup and the simple syrup to taste. Shake well. Strain into a chilled martini glass. To garnish, float three coffee beans on the top of the drink.

NUTS ABOUT COFFEE

INGREDIENTS

1 ounce whole milk

1 ounce heavy cream

1¼ ounces strong cold
espresso coffee

¼ ounce caramel syrup

1 tablespoon orgeat

Grated chocolate,
to garnish

ADD A TWIST

Whisky or rum would add
extra depth of flavor to
this martini.

The nuts in this case are almonds; the almond flavor itself is contained in the syrup that goes by the name orgeat. For the taste profile of this drink to work, the coffee needs to be strong, hence the use of espresso. You may choose to use a little less caramel syrup as the orgeat is also quite sweet.

METHOD

Fill a martini glass with crushed ice to chill it. While it's chilling, add all of the ingredients to an ice-filled cocktail shaker. Shake well. Remove the ice from the martini glass; it should be nicely frosted. Fine-strain into the martini glass. Garnish with chocolate (white, dark, or milk—your choice) grated over top.

8 PITCHER PARTY

PREP AND PRE-PARTY PLANNING

Let's say you have six to eight dinner guests and will have an hour of drinks before food is served. Practice making your drink from start to finish. You need to know how long it takes you to make one before you set about making a number of them for several (waiting) guests. This is also an excellent way to be certain you have all the right equipment, ingredients, glassware, and garnishes. Think of it as your trial run. Glasses, too, can be garnished in advance, so you have an effortless transition from one style of drink to the next.

If you're setting out a number of drinks on a bar surface or table, to greet guests as they arrive, arrange them in a circle or other shape. If the occasion is to honor an individual or a couple, how about laying the glasses out to form their initial(s)?

So now you know what you're making, how you're going to embellish and present it, you just need to know how many people you are making each drink for. Most recipes are for one person, though I have included a few punches in this chapter that are good for groups.

Enjoy shaking, stirring, and blending your way through this collection of fun, colorful, and tasty alcohol-free cocktails. Cheers and good health!

CHOOSING RECIPES

Don't give your guests anything too outlandish. Something not too sharp or too sweet is a good starting point. Remember: First impressions matter. Choose a recipe heavy on the "wow" factor: It should look as good as it tastes. A garnish of bright strawberry red and deep lime green provide a nice stark contrast. Make sure there's enough fresh ice in the drinks. Be sure to stir the drinks as you hand them out. Everyone likes the refreshing sound of ice clinking against the side of the glass. It also signals the amount of care you've put into every aspect of composing the drink—from choosing the freshest ingredients to making sure its taste hasn't been watered down. Before your first guest has even taken a sip, you will have already appealed to four of the five senses: the colorful garnish elicits the sense of sight; the smell of fresh fruit hanging in the air teases the nose; the clinking of the ice perks up the ears; and the refreshingly cold glass pleasantly sparks the sensation of touch.

If you'll need to serve another drink and want to vary things a little, a punch is good for the next offering as you can have the whole bowl or pitcher already made up, leaving only ice to be added at the last minute.

Dairy drinks are often a suitable accompaniment to desserts, whereas the sharpness of a citrusy drink makes a great aperitif. It goes without saying that nonalcoholic versions of classics make for the ideal party beverage. Although most ingredients are available online (or in today's well-stocked supermarkets) year-round, there are still foods and flavors we associate with certain times of year, so do try using "seasonal" ingredients.

PRETTY AS A PITCHER

SERVES 6

INGREDIENTS

7 ounces (1 cup) raspberries

5 ounces pear juice

Juice from 3 limes

33 ounces ginger beer

Handful raspberries and
    slices of lime, to garnish

ADD A TWIST

Vodka or gin work nicely
with the fruit flavors here.

As its name suggests, this is a drink to be prepared and served by the pitcher.

Technically, raspberries aren't fruit but, instead, come from the rose family, of which there are over two hundred varieties. High in fiber and low in calories, raspberries contain more vitamin C than oranges.

METHOD

Wash the raspberries and blend with the pear juice. Fill a pitcher half full of crushed ice. Add the lime juice. Pour the blended raspberry and pear mix into the pitcher. Top with ginger beer, and drop whole raspberries into the drink. Make sure everyone gets at least one raspberry in their ice-filled glass. Garnish with a slice of lime on the rim of each glass.

LEMON REFRESHER

SERVES 12

INGREDIENTS:

28 ounces (4 cups) sugar

7 ounces (1 cup) fresh
    mint leaves

17 ounces fresh lemon juice

8½ cups soda water

4 fresh limes

Sprig of mint and slices
    of lemon, to garnish

This fabulous summer punch is ideally served in a glass punchbowl to show off its vivid greens and yellows.

The mint-infused simple syrup requires a bit of preparation. Best to plan in advance.

METHOD

Boil a kettle full of water and put a heavy-based pan on the heat. Pour the boiling water into the pan. Add the sugar; it will take only a minute or two for the sugar to dissolve completely. Turn off the heat to let cool. Once the mixture is at room temperature, add the mint leaves and stir well into the sugar-water. Leave overnight to infuse.

The next day, put a dozen ice cubes into a punchbowl. Add the lemon juice, and pour in the sugar-water. Top with soda. Chop the limes into quarters and squeeze the juice into the punch. Ladle into ice-filled handled jars. Garnish each drink with a sprig of mint and a slice of lemon.

WATERMELON & BASIL COOLER

SERVES 6

INGREDIENTS

20 large fresh basil leaves,
   plus 6 to garnish
1 watermelon
5 ounces still water, chilled
Juice from 1 lime
6 slices of lime, to garnish

The hardest part about making this drink is preparing the watermelon; it requires some effort to cut it into smaller pieces for blending. The best part of this drink may be its aroma of fresh lime and basil. A summer mix like this begs to be served alongside a picnic of sandwiches and fresh fruits.

METHOD

Place the basil leaves in a large glass jug. Carve the watermelon into boats first and then carve out the sections. Cut thinly so you can pop out the seeds with the point of a knife. Don't worry if you can't extract all of the seeds. Do your best to preserve as much of the fruit's flesh as possible.

Blend the watermelon with the water, lime juice, and a few ice cubes. Pour into a large glass jug. Muddle the basil leaves against the inside of the jug. Stir well. Pour into highball glasses filled with crushed ice. Stick the leftover basil leaves into the slices of lime and garnish.

FRUIT TEA REFRESHER

SERVES 4

INGREDIENTS

2 herbal fruit tea bags of
   your choice
1 cinnamon stick
1 vanilla pod
Grated orange zest
5 tellicherry peppercorns
1 tablespoon ginger cordial
1 ounce fresh lemon juice
¼ ounce simple syrup
1 raspberry; 1 sprig of mint;
   and 1 piece of fresh
   ginger, to garnish

Best made as a large batch due to the amount of work that goes into the making. Even though you're making a large batch, serve and garnish each drink separately, as the garnishes add a fair bit to the overall drink.

You can vary the type of fruit tea used.

METHOD

Brew the tea. Add the cinnamon stick, vanilla pod, grated orange zest, and tellicherry peppercorns to the teapot. Leave to cool and infuse. Strain the cold tea into an ice-filled cocktail shaker. Add the ginger cordial, lemon juice, and simple syrup. Shake well. Strain into an ice-filled Casablanca glass. Peel the skin off the ginger before placing it in the drink next to a sprig of mint and a raspberry perched on the edge of the glass.